COMEBACK

Poems in Conversation
1984–1989

Peter Esterhuysen
&
Paul Mason

BODHI BOOKS

With special thanks to
Silke Heiss and Eduard Burle

ACKNOWLEDGEMENTS
'Close encounters', 'paren(theses) and 'Students talk (1984)' first
appeared in *Imago* (11), 1986, pp 5, 12 and 17. 'The Man in the poem'
first appeared in *Soundings*, edited by Douglas Reid-Skinner, Cape Town,
Carrefour Press, 1989. A number of these poems appeared on the internet
website *Off the Wall Poetry* Western Cape, 9 April 2007, pp 9–18.

Published by Bodhi Books, 6 Africander Road, Murdoch Valley,
Simon's Town, 7975

Initial layout by Dean Fourie, Source Corporation
DTP by User Friendly
Cover art by Silke Heiss
Photographs by Silke Heiss, Deirdre Byrne, Amanda Esterhuysen, Nika
Raphaely and Mary Raphaely

Contents

REMEMBERING
PETER

For Peter Jonathan Esterhuysen
(20 June 1963–9 April 2004)

and Nika Raphaely

Prelude

In the title of this compilation of poems I have contracted 'come' and 'back' from the well-known nursery rhyme to say something truthful about Peter Esterhuysen. Throughout his life he staged comebacks. During our university years bouts of illness would consign him to bed. But his bed became an alternative empire from which he held forth while gesturing expansively, urging friends and himself on to the next book, play, film or piece of music. It might be said that his innate theatricality achieved its climax with his departure on Good Friday 2004. Who else would have had the audacity to upstage the Christ figure?! Perhaps he sensed that such a choice of departure time presaged yet another comeback? And here it is.

The core of this book revives the poetic dialogue in which the two of us were engaged from the mid- to the late 1980s. By doing so I am paying tribute not only to Peter, but to what was integral to his work and life: the crafting of words.

In the mid-80s Peter wrote a poem in which he looked back on his undergraduate years in the early 80s, years in which formative friendships were established –

Crossing the piazza (in terza stanza)

That first meeting was accidental,
incidental, or so it seemed then;

providential (as those of a romantic disposition
might describe it), undoubtedly consequential;

one day while crossing a cement piazza
we unexpectedly crystallised into each other.

The poem's title is a direct response to poems I wrote at that time. But the content, I have no doubt, speaks not only to

Peter's lover of that time, but to many of his friends. It certainly reminds me of my first meeting with him in the Law Library at Wits University in 1983. That meeting, and the friendship that followed, played a significant part in the two of us dropping Law in favour of studying and working with words.

'Remembering Peter' consists of an Obituary, and my poetic tribute written shortly after his death. 'Echoes' contains selected poems from our dialogue of 1984–1989, and 'Two Poems' (2006) resonates with the presence of Peter (the two of us shared affinities for the myth of Sisyphyus, as well as for the charm of 'half moons').

pm

A quiet hero blessed with a gift for storytelling

OBITUARY: PETER ESTERHUYSEN

Peter Esterhuysen was born with cystic fibrosis and was not expected to see his 20th birthday. Instead he lived to become the oldest person with severe cystic fibrosis in South Africa, fighting a determined and ingenious war with the debilitating condition.

He was a quiet hero blessed with a gift for storytelling. He created wonderful educational comics, TV/film scripts, school textbooks, plays and much, much more. As a literacy activist and teacher, Esterhuysen's passion and vision were to create a popular culture of reading for pleasure and knowledge for ordinary South Africans, using the medium of comics.

Together with Neil Napper he founded the StoryTeller Group for this purpose. He pioneered in situ workshops with his target audience where he listened to hundreds of anecdotes and conflicting voices. Working against the legacy of monolithic and monologic apartheid policies, he believed that if stories contained multiple voices and views, they created dialogue and spaces for discussion. Fundamental to the methods he developed was a deep respect for his reader.

StoryTeller's first publication was *River of our Dreams* (1990), a comic on environmental health. StoryTeller had a strong commitment to multilingualism at a time when very few publishers had thought about it. There followed many highly successful comics, including *Heart to Heart*, which explored gender, power and sexuality in a rural setting, and *Love and Aids*, one of the first HIV/Aids education publications.

After *Spider's Place*, a multimedia project on Science Education with Handspring Puppet Company, Esterhuysen was invited to the famous Muppet studios in New York.

Deep Cuts (1993) was a groundbreaking adaptation to comic of short stories by three South African writers: Can Themba, Bessie Head and Alex la Guma.

Esterhuysen's emphasis on dialogue extended to his work in TV and he was influential in developing South African "edutainment". A key contribution was his ability to map compelling stories and vivid character journeys, against social and political complexities, across a whole television series. He wrote for *Soul City, Gazlam* and *Yizo Yizo* series I and II. He anchored the writing team and, while others focused on depicting the grit and violence of township life, he maintained the human depth and complexity of the characters.

Yizo Yizo won multiple awards both locally and internationally, including the Japan and Geneva prizes for best TV drama. Esterhuysen was not properly credited for his contribution, and although deeply hurt, he never became negative but always looked ahead, developing the next project. In 2002 he co-wrote a feature film with Tebogo Mahlatsi called *Scar*, the story of two friends affected by hostel violence. The script was selected for the Sundance Writers Laboratory in Utah, which he was too ill to attend.

Esterhuysen was his own multidisciplinary healer, combining conventional medicine and alternative therapies to great effect. He was an expert on cystic fibrosis, way ahead of his doctors, whom he generally guided. He did not consider himself a victim, but chose to live life to the full. Inconceivably, in his late thirties he was diagnosed with another genetic disease, a familial leukaemia. His courage was astonishing.

The one single word that describes Esterhuysen is "humanity": only this can embrace his many qualities and convey the depth to which he possessed them. He had "guts", he was a fighter who never allowed his illness to set limits on his zest for life, to impinge on his dignity or to interfere in his relations with others. People were the centre of his life and he had the talent of being able to connect with anyone. He was wise, generous, tender and mischievous and his gentle wit taught us all to laugh at ourselves.

He died on April 9 and will be missed by his wife, sister, parents and friends.
Barak Morgan

Peter Jonathan Esterhuysen, born 1963, died April 9 2004

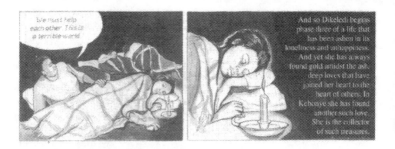

A wreath of sixty-five roses*

pc (1984)

Pale and thin,
white, delicate-veined
with bunched stalks –
they droop in the sun.
The diseased fruit of a mismarriage.
Or was it the season?
The climate? The ground?
'Sixty-five roses, how quaint',
she murmurs,
'for an illness'.

I draw into the shadows of a word
that has hung over me throughout my life,
filtering and shaping the attitudes
of those around me.
Unarticulated, it was a misfortune,
articulated, it is a curse.
'Sixty-five roses',
she intones.
The distance between us is sufficient
for her benediction to become unintelligible,
a suitable epitaph.

---

*Sixty-five roses is a euphemism for cystic fibrosis.

A common calling

pm (2004)

I write. I stop.
I write again.

The years have bent me,
my feet give me pain as I walk.

The years – forty of them – have bent me
a little.
My feet protest when I walk
a lot.

I return from a bench that stands at the edge
of a dam, in front of a yellowwood sapling.
On a brass plaque attached to the bench
are these words: '… when we walked
it was with eyes beneath our feet,
mind full of the sun, the grass
and the cleaving dust-red path' –
words by, and for, my dead friend.
I write for him.
I wrote with him.

We scan photographs of him for the memorial service.
In these is the full smile,
the brown-eyed brimming zest of one
told as a child he would not live
beyond twenty.
At forty he has gone now from us.
We enlarge the photographs. Doing so
says something about him:
he was larger than his own life,
larger than the limits of his body.

In being so he was
larger than life itself.
What is left behind?
What remains to remind us?

Us.
The us that bowed down together
to a common cause, a common calling:
words: their shaping.

1987, during one of the States of Emergency,
we wrote a play together.
I had unearthed an old poem of mine
about a man put on trial for his dreams.
We plotted it, tweaking at its strands and ligaments,
twanging at its chords,
dancing on the eggs of its newness,
prancing around the theatre's lobby,
two wet-behind-the-ears dramaturgists making
verbal turgidities spring to a life (of sorts).
Our parents watched it with (unspoken) pride.
We watched it with prematurely jaundiced eyes.
Neither of us liked it. The script, called
Dream Court, took legs and walked away
from its only three nights on this earth,
never to be recreated.
Years later
we joked about resurrecting it.

We wrote poetry in separate cities.
Our words interwove,
fed into and out of each other.
They visited, they called upon,
they circumnavigated and circumscribed
each other.

They concocted a common exile,
took refuge in their own shadows.
They were beautiful in their doings together,
their mourning the mornings,
their me-in-him-ings, their him-in-me-ings,
their hymnings forth
of the common calling.

During the next State of Emergency
I returned to your city. There,
in your commune, we sat with friends
on a double mattress, ears tuned to our poems until,
suddenly, we heard splintering of glass,
then footfalls. Alert, fearful, ears pricked
to other sounds. Footfalls neared as our eyes
fixed on the door. You heeded the common gaze,
rose and locked us in. Sitting, breathing raggedly, listening …
Then George – the boldest among us –
(nearing the moment of his exile) rose,
unlocked the door, and went down the passageway.
In the front room he met the intruder,
opened the door for him
and gestured that he depart.
Instead the man turned hastily,
pulled down a panga decorating the wall,
and attacked.
Later we visited George
in the casualties unit with bloodied head
and a story to take away with him.

That 'pangaman incident',
though nothing more than incident,
marked the end of a time,
our time. We moved on
from those selves that had
enjoyed a common calling.

There came other times to re-enchant,
to salve, our renewed selves.
We made time for each other within
our new worlds.
My eyes linger on a photograph
from one such time: we two on my bed,
jesting, performing our mock-
erotic gestures,
our hugs and almost-kisses:
the reality of our affection.

Then followed a time
things fell apart for me.
I got into a rusted car and drove
to the harbour of your home.
There we talked, ate liquorice toffees,
stayed up late, tuned our bodies
at the local gym, revisited our *ennui*.
Listening together to *The Song of Being a Child*,
we regained something of our child-days,
remembered an energy
that lived inside those days –
something that had moved us,
that we saw and knew in each other
when first we met half our life-times ago.

In a recent dream I sit in a lecture theatre.
The person at the rostrum announces
that someone is absent: you.
We await you, but the lecture must commence.
The air bristles with your absence.
Then, with a flourish, you arrive.
People in the back row
beckon to you. I call out your name
as you ascend the steps.
You give a hasty smile.

And now the chase is on,
for you move at a pace like no other.
This is your nature, born from Marvell's truth:
'Always at my back I hear
Time's winged chariot hurrying near ...'
You are pulled in several directions
by many at once. To have time
with you I must pursue, harry,
commandeer, hijack a slice of it.
When you are cornered, settled down,
the pay-off resonates.
Something intense and rich surfaces:
a subtext of knowing
between one and the other.

I knew you. You knew me.
This will never not be.
It is –
though you aren't
with us any longer.

Still I dream, with comforting regularity,
of you. You reappear,
become manifest,
again and again and
again ...

ECHOES

poems by Peter & Paul

(1984–1989)

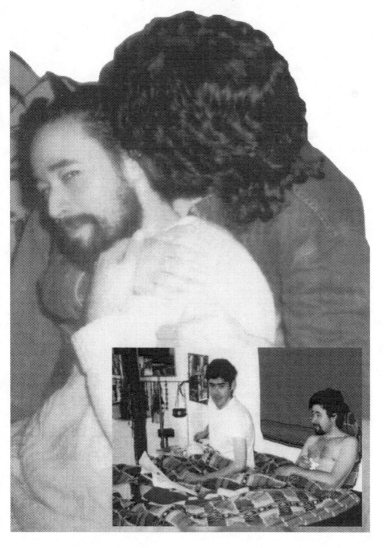

Prologue

Our body is the bodhi* tree,
and our mind a mirror bright.
Carefully we wipe them hour by hour,
and let no dust alight.

—o—

There is no bodhi tree,
nor stand of mirror bright,
since all is void,
where can the dust alight?

*The tree under which Buddha sat and attained enlightenment.

From *The Little Zen Companion*, by David Schiller, p. 121
Stanza 1 written by monks in the monastery of the Fifth Patriarch,
Hung-jen
Stanza 2 written by Hui-neng, kitchen helper in the above monastery, later
to become the Sixth Patriarch

It is

It is the mezuzah on your doorframe,
it is the rearview mirror in your stationary car,
it is the light reflected in your fanlight.

It is also the vision from the landlocked boat
of the lit window behind which you stand, you
who are unknown to me, on the twenty-fifth floor.

It is the mezuzah,
it is the rear-view mirror,
it is the light,
it is also the vision
of the lit window
on the twenty-fifth floor.

Finally it is the distance between
the landlocked boat and the window
as the light goes out
and I watch you recline.

It isn't

It isn't the mezuzah on your doorframe,
it isn't the spy-hole's vacant gaze,
it isn't the light-web in your fanlight
and it isn't your outline in a window on the twenty-fifth floor.
Lippitude settled in four beers ago, blotting out
your window, the land-locked boat and the distance between:
but when your light dies do you stare briefly
at the street-singed fog below and wonder
if the same breath that clouds your rear-view
disturbs the mezuzah when the room shudders?

Ah, it isn't the mezuzah,
it isn't the eye's spy,
it isn't the rear-view mirror,
nor is it the vision
of the unlit window
on the twenty-fifth floor
that draws me to your door.

I's images

I rise from my desk and its books
and stand in the doorway
facing night's chill,
room's warmth behind me.

A score of headlights rounds
the vanishing-point of the land
as it skirts the sea.
I project my mind beyond the series of twin-lights
to the successive lives behind them.
I step back and muse at length,
on the negative power of multiplicity.

At a particular turn
each beam that's cast
cuts the sea's dark face
in a scar of light.

My mind weaves its moments in a flickering trace:
from each imagined life that imagines itself
to be free, to the distance between
them and me, to what I imagine myself to be.

I relinquish the looming chill of the night
for the adumbrated horizon of my room.
I am unable to resume my books,
my former resolve rendered desolate
by the image of all those others
who are each saying I, just like me

(that is, the me I imagine myself to be).

a poem about myself

who am I?
unburied self I try
to conceal from
those who pry?
or the me I wear
from day to day –
capricious mask
in pliant clay?
Everyone has a part
in designing my face,
yet 'I' seems such a private spot
for so public a place.

Hymn to myself

I return through the garden,
observe the silent rituals. Genuflect
at the bank of the stream, bend
to watch the reeds move, listen
to their rhythmic clatter in the breeze.

Rise and stretch, and move on, over
the footbridge and up the steps mossed-over,
to the terrace of green with
the pond at its centre. Then up
to the rice paper house, its transparency.
It is the only house,
I know it well, am its only occupant.
Always the same, all in its place ...

You have never lived in it:
to this it owes its ... stasis.

But who has lived in it?
Who has seen to its perpetuity?

He has,
that other one –

renouncing the garden and its rituals,
descending upon no knee, watching
no reeds, crossing
no footbridge, up
no mossed-over steps, across
no terrace with its pond, to
no rice paper house and
its abstract occupancy.

A place that is nothing,
all-changing.

A blossom. Multifoleate.
No, not even.
Nothing.

Don't breathe a word of it,
lest they know.
Don't speak my name when I am gone.
Give me no quarter, brook me no consequences.
See me as death, treat me as such.
Be oblivious of me and kind to others:
renounce me.
Certify me unspeakable
to be loved by all.
Permit me no reed
on which to pluck my posthumous tune.
Never upturn the moss that entombs me.
Take me nowhere with you.
Leave me still,
unchanging.
Renounce me.

Speak me.
Breathe my every word.
Inspire and expire me.
Be incessantly my Annunciation's angel.
See me ever-emerging, all-reaching.
Sanctify my word and breath.
Be my life and death.
Be me.

Yet another poem about myself

To my apperceiving glance
your marrying stare con-
jugates what I appear
to you to be and the you-
ness that so defines me:

there is a coupling in
your eyes like water
in air, soaking up the
spaces but also ef-
facing an absence.

Why do I fear this
blank in my amness,
and fill up the blue
with other eyes?

Dawn's blush

Beneath dawn's blush
a flush-burst bauble
shimmers and moons
into mourning –
our lives are mitred
by risings, by leavings,
swayed by streams of traffic –
single in cars but not alone.
Single in cars (to recap a metaphor)
but always lonely,
we scratch the sleep from our eyes
and try to forget the traffic
that edges out of view
never to double back
beneath the blush,
the flush-burst bauble
that shimmers and moons
into morning.

The poet and the underwriting

> Be strange to me.
> I am tired of outward forms,
> listless in similarity,
> paralysed by monotony,
> bored with my proliferating selves
> And my words spiral ...
> away from me.
>
> The poet.

The guns will be strange.
The sjamboks and people rising
from crouched positions
in hidden places will be strange,
will tear reality into being
and cup the inner voice
in the outward show
of clenched fists
and the inarticulate cry.

The dead bodies will be strange,
will underwrite every word
with an unyielding solidity,
for there can be little ambiguity
in poetry of the coldest,
most naked flesh.

The poets most of all,
most of all, will be strange,
will die desperate deaths

when all their spun phrases
take sudden turns
and metaphors need be ripped
from the guts.

And then will their cries,
will their fearful cries,
be any stranger
than the rest?

A kind of lament

Too many smoke-encrusted evenings,
too many blurred peripheries
and clotted visions,
and too, too many plastic-red beaks
glinting,
dipping to tear and raven the carcass
of morning.

Between sky and sea

I saw a Pyrenese mountain dog
walking beneath the moon
between the sky and sea.

The moon was orange as it sunk
to the sea, and cast its glow
in light-points leaping
to the rock, where I sat
only minutes ago.

Where I sat and hovered …
between heart's stirrings and
mind's icy intercessions
there swelled the first motions
of an edgeless fear that took firmer hold

as moon set and
sky and sea
blackened.

I sat on heavily,
heard a soft shuffle,
then a noise behind me. My nerves stretched taut.
Strange days, I thought. Stroked my chin,
appeared to muse,
despite the rising fear of being

ended

on that rock.

I beat a hasty retreat,
crossed the street,
ascended
the first steps homeward,
glanced back over my shoulder.

It was then that

I saw a Pyrenese mountain dog
walking beneath the moon
between the sky and sea.

Pen and patriarchy

Once a figure enough to provoke silence
and fear, and love,
that towered over me and stood firmly,
root-secure in the earth.
Now he sits, smaller, shorter
and shrinking whenever I turn my back –
there is no longer the fear,
only the silence lingers still.

Now unprovoked, perhaps softer,
it is the silence of rarified air,
where words echo themselves
out of existence
and a numbness of pain
unarticulated remains.
Sometimes I turn to face him
and the silence echoes with silent echoes
of numberless, accusing cries:
father what have you fathered?
Only silence returns the silent answer.

Locomotive

Time and space out there
come surging in here –
the train like a Cyclops
with myriad faces inside that look out,
or one face a hundred times
fragmented.
As I look in they look out,
framed each by windows that rhyme
with the clatter of wheels on the track.

I know what few of them
learn from their mirrors –
that the railway timetable lives
inside them. Head and heart, wheels
on the track, we cannot go back.
We cannot go back.

Finger-painting
for Judy

In motion,
a hand that stirs the water
and hair that runs untrammelled,
merging with the leaves
and the broken lines
of a pale and watery portrait:
suddenly tossed back
to catch the wind and ripples
in the curve
of an arc,
moment of infinite
possibility.
Tide and gesture
move and merge
with life as stillness,
acquiescent;
and then a lowering,
with hair streaming down.
A convergence
into softest clarity,
ripples subside
in the wake
of trailing fingers.

paren(theses)

(fuck-all matters anyway)
you greet the dusk you greet the day
(it all comes it all goes)
you pick the weed you pick the rose
(the sun will shine the sun will set)
you make hay you forget
(the moon will wax the moon will wane)
you live the joy you live the pain
(love will give love will refuse)
you win the game the game you lose
(the life will rise the life will fall)
you fly you crawl
(the point is there the point is gone)
you can't go on you go on
(the laurels of victory the thorns of defeat)
you excrete the shit the shit you eat
(the dusk that falls the break of day)
fuck-all matters anyway

Welcome to this poem

Welcome
to this poem,
make yourself at home.
Would you care for something
refreshing, some light relief?
A cup of tea perhaps?
You must be exhausted reading
all those poems out there,
and when one thinks of the unfigured
multitude (can you bear
the thought?) cross-breeding in bottom drawers …

It is a long, bitter winter's night and who dares
be an arbiter of taste in times like these?
And — oh the poet?
He's not in today,
He's out selling life.
The big companies pay
well, not forgetting the benefits,
and they love him
when he is angry.

Poem

Heaving ungainly at tomorrow:
futile some say,
others say festive.
I wonder: what's in
the running to be gainsaid,
where the instruments
at our disposal with which
to glue our time to the backcloth
and make it, somehow, signify?

I harbour no hard-and-fast notions
in this or any other regard,
in this of all places. Just
to know of frail small sprouts
splitting the earth to don daylight:
both festive and futile,
unfurling.

a new word

i learned a new word yesterday;
i was searching for another word
to express the darkness and
deep, mole-sighted arrogance of
some white people I have met in this country;
the word I needed was immitigable,
for actions beyond the pale of understanding,
but stumbled instead on immolate: to offer in sacrifice –

somehow they go together, complete
on the verge of an amnesia

blinder than words,
thicker than death.

A lover's lament

Something snaked in some
where between us (beware
they said of the pools)
so we watched our pools,
fastening the straps (do not go barefoot
they said) and when we
walked it was with eyes
beneath our feet, mind
full of the sun, the grass
and the cleaving dust-red
path (in summer search your
tracks); perhaps it was
merely an ash-coloured, winter
inch (snakes they said) worm.

Close encounters

I bring you poisonous flowers,
I kiss your sister's hand.

I bring you poisonous flowers,
you say thank-you as you walk by.
I kiss your sister's hand
and stroke her flaxen hair.

You say how sweet
as you place my flowers in the bin

while I talk with your sister
about breathing.

Elegy in pronouns

You and I (lost in the
amorphousness of we
and us) are, in our conjunction,
half the sum of our former
selves (and halfness has become
the water-mark of our
partiality).

(Joined together at weaker
points) we form a new relief
and (fixed in this tightening
completeness) are no longer
able to trace the pencil-line
cracks,

the thread of light
that glimmered
between us: you and
amorphousness.

The poet is addressed by his public

We are glad you are st
ill with us. Your
kind is necess
ary. If things
were to hap
pen differently, you
may well find your
self reaping the bene
fits of a bounteo
us harvest. As it
stands however, and
as an auth
or, you have the opport
unity, in this busy world,
of capitalising on the bound
less material
offalled to, correction, off
erred to you by soci

The man in the poem

The man in the poem you wrote
inclined his head, cleared his throat,
bent to see the time. He said
have the children been fed? He said
are they ready for bed?

No children to feed, they've gone out to play,
they said there is going to be a carnival today.
The streets are barricaded, buses on fire,
they are piling the rubbish higher and higher.
I said I saw them building a funeral pyre.

We're living on the edge, he said, of a pirouette,
we'll all go spinning to our graves yet,
will it ever wind down? I shook my head.
Only when all the fires have been fed, I said,
or when the turning hand has fled.

Streets below

Day's vision telescopes
in headlong gaze at
rain dismal above the ocean.

It is the perspective, staggered,
foreshortened, from there till
here where we sit, that offends
clarity, that thickens
to clog mind's passages
and the passages that recede are
dimmed each beyond any
point of knowing, such that
all residua are reflections,
all motions shadows.

There were murmurs that
dropped from pretty railings to
streets below alive with people.

There were murmurs, and there
were people. These are gone.
There was love. It is dead
as the street.

There

for George who procrastinated before going into exile

To watch, to wait,
to wait again;
waiting confirms and
disturbs the face-splashed
surface as somewhere
the air breathes
and a leaf clatters
to the ground, disturbs
as a fly buzzes somewhere
and thumps dully against
the glass, confirms as the roof
cracks somewhere, as you move
to the window where a solitary
tree breaks the surface
without even moving, and as
the ripples wheel with widening arms,
breaks the eye's tensile film
as the ripples wheel and widen,
breaks the face's tensive watching
without even moving,
breaks the surface with

the weight
        of waiting.

Exhibits

Like the mind anaesthetised,
locked between sleep and
the expectation of pain;

like the unborn,
the unliving foetus,
macabrely animated in the
dull liquid of the jar.

Lines

Her wrists are laced with little lines, he says
of a friend who has problems living. I think of her
pallid skin, tautened, tightening as her hand
twists back into a bow and the little blocks
shrink and multiply with each deft graving.
I am reminded of a street map
of a rapidly growing suburb.
It is easy to imagine
between arteries of such busy traffic:
the tree-lined houses, the well-kept gardens,
little children, happy couples, postboxes,
a bicycle or two, stop streets,
pylons and lines – miles of wire

crossing the corpuscular sky.

Manifesto from the crepuscular colony (during internal exile)

There is the dull constant flow with odd irruptions. For the sake of ease and consistency let us call these irruptions visions. Such visions are not to be forgotten: the motions of sun and socius be damned! It's in the twilight that we know what everyone, including ourselves, forgets during the daylight. So we sleep through the days and awaken at twilight.

Wakefulness: the light that floods in to dispel our dreams and institute the Dominion of Actions. Our enforced enlistment to this Dominion has never shown us any visions with lives larger than those of its funereal regime. Our petty diurnals have been like those of all the others who at this very moment fulgurate toward the half-light like amoebae.

Visions are known only while lying awake in the dark with foghorns signaling invisible mists. For the seafarer these are clarions of danger. For we, inhabitants of this crepuscular colony, they are signs of either hard or gentle melancholy, of surprising comfort or unremitting desolation (depending on the promptness of milk and postal deliveries, and such like).

Sometimes a flock of geese might fly overhead and this, commingling with the foghorn, is quite agreeable. We rise to piss, but go straight back to bed. There is nothing to be done today.

i went to your poems in search of a flower
for Wally Serote

i went to your poems in search of a flower
to press between the pages of some book
as my grandmother used to do (she was
an innocent and never knew beyond her pages,
the flowers of Sharpeville never died for her
and perhaps they were never born).
But your beds had been ravaged,
your earth was moist with water-
green, headless stalks turning
brown within putrescent
leaves (when she died i searched
her pages for something preserved
but found only the yellow-grained
remnants of fish-moths staining
the crumbling pages). I will come again
in another season, brother, you
must not cut down the flowers, remember
the nature of our oppression will always
be smaller than the aesthetic of our anger.

Having waited in launderettes
and at bus-stops

We alien few
sad aesthetes
who have insisted,
in all company, on
the primacy of the word;

they who have lived
outside of our insistence,
in spite of our vision,
who have never taken us
at our word;

we who move in spite
of their wordlessness,
they in spite of our words,
in the same streets
through the same hours.

When in Brakpan

The Casbah in Brakpan
serves raspberry-red milkshakes
in vase-size glasses
just flash your lights
for service and don't hesitate
to move closer when the car in front
drives away and don't forget
the tray clasped to your window
when you drive away and it is
probably not wise to stare
at the khaki figures lined up
knocking back the shakes in
the casspirs at Casbah in Brakpan.

Occupation

Spend years learning how to become something:
then become it: that's it then:
dentist: lawyer: optometrist:
that's it: decay and putrefaction:
pictures on the desk or on the walls of the office:
the reasons and the motives frozen like the photographs
        cut to fit the frames:
that's employment: the ossifying of intentions:
shaping the means to fit the ends:
then the mould sets and the means cease to matter:
then the ritual and the repetition:
actions formulated: motives, means and ends encapsulated:
concentrated in the necessary relations:
patients and clients:
then there are the instruments:
the instruments become the life:
the life becomes the instruments:
drill bits and polishers:
contracts and statutes:
optics and eye charts:
that's the pattern then:
and so it goes:
gum disease and tooth decay:
libel and delictual damages:
spectacles and contact lenses:
that's the pattern that follows employment:
decay:
occupation itself:
that's the occupational hazard.

Blood in the suburbs

That was the year of the bleeding sun
that parched the earth
and flayed the sky;
and old men threw bones
in their well-kept backyards,
bent double in unconscious homage
before the merciless African heat.

And the scorched grass shrivelled;
and the flowers all died
in the suffocating embrace
of what seemed to be a single afternoon.
While the algae-free garden ponds, stained
by the sun's reflection,
implicated their ornate surroundings

And everything else reflected;
and yellow-bearded gnomes,
with cracked, concrete smiles,
frowned in the whites of their eyes,
indignant, it would seem,
at the very thought of blood
reaching the suburbs.

Your white wedding

You went for counselling sessions
for weeks before this day,
and today you wear your white dress
in front of this priest. I too see your white dress
from where I sit amid the congregation,
but I see it differently: covered by the snail-trails
of all your spirited couplings, soiled
by the exclamations from your lover's lively cock.
Your lover now your husband in the sanctity
of this Union, each subsequent union
accorded God's mandate, rendered sacred
from this day forth.

After the ceremony I approach
your priest and ask – 'How'd you enjoy
being fucked in the eye?'

The growing

Our resident lives
lived in close spaces
with squares of grass
measured by mowers
fed on diluted sun
and watered-down tea
and cautious fantasies

where trains and traffic passing by
drown our plaintive cries
when our fantasies erupt
and take form like
bulbous heads mush-
rooming out of rain.

In October the creepers bleed
and the saucers stare back
with saurian eyes
while in concealed backyards
this is the season
of the chimeras breeding
amongst the slugs and snails.

Students talk (1984)

We sat in a centreless
circle, sipping tea and
liqueurs between snippets

of concerned conversation.
She (of feminist persuasion)
talked of 'boring liberal'

issues such as rape, abortion,
prostitution, and of weightier
issues like militant lesbianism.

He (of firm persuasions)
spoke of the Internal Security
Act, detentions, forced removals;

and we all discussed the
campus base (keeping, of course,
our throats lubricated with

liqueurs); and our conversation
shifted to Europe and the
cheapest means of travel.

Then we spoke of student
ideals, their tenuous nature
when confronting the 'outside

world', and though often
I (of unsettled persuasion)
wonder at their detached

involvement and feel sometimes
pride, sometimes shame, at my
own deeper detachment, I wonder

also if we will ever be free
in that outside world to
talk in this way about 'issues'.

Students talk (1987)

We sat in high-backed chairs:
the seminar was under way.
Codes: the need to differentiate

between the proiaretic, the hermeneutic
and the semic: alienation increases
exponentially with each deft differentiation.

Then we remove to an informal setting
for a supper of fish and vegetables.
We speak of the libidinal philosophers,

of problems of praxis, of ideology's
attenuation of agency. We eat fish and
drink wine. I note the newspaper headline

before the page is absently turned:
'Reef violence: 6 men killed, 16 000
strikers fired.' On the same page

Botha proclaims 'I am a democrat'.
Conversation resumes and while they speak
I recall that Althusser strangled his wife,

Poulantzas committed suicide, Barthes
was run over by a bus. And while often I
wonder at their detached involvement through

'issues' with the 'outside world', I feel
no pride, only shame, at my own detachment.
I do not know how to be in either world.

A fellow-student asks for a lift home. I'm
going his direction and it's an excuse
to leave. In the car he speaks of the issue

of intellectual versus populist raised by the
recent formation of a grassroots newspaper
and says 'I have never made claims to being

a worker'. He seems to know what he is. Back
home sitting at my desk I read the stories
in full – 'Reef violence: 6 men killed,

16 000 strikers fired', and on the same page:
'Botha – government busy on reform'. I read on,
make a sandwich, lie awake till morning

breaks on another day in which I will sit in a
high-backed chair, considering the structure of
narratives, reading the newspaper over a cup of tea.

Photographs

I sometimes see faces
once loved, but now lost,
with expressions that edge
the odd moments that measure a life.

And when we meet now
it is as strangers, though more familiar still.
I search for some passing likeness
of a you without to a you within.
But it is difficult to frame
a face that is closed –
already turned away.
It is easier to part.
Neither of us have cause to stay.

Paper leaves, burning brown at their edges,
fall as I walk in measured steps,
and unfocused fingers frame space to admit,
in a moment of smoke-filled silence,
the mystery in lost causes.

Writing on Evening

Sun sunk down
behind grey-striated,
ink-scarred sky
alive again with
another dying lie:
that blank-black
night descends at
day's end. It
does not descend,
it falls hard
and is dumbly
resisted. But then,
all nature is
dumb, like the
stilled tongue, like
the expectant pen.

Blood

I have felt your blood on my hands.
I remember it well,
staring at the watery redness
as it dried on my skin,
leaving a stain
between my outspread fingers
held up to the light.
And I remember thinking
of natural cycles,
of the earth,
of procreation;
and of how to express feelings
that I ought to be feeling:
such as distaste
at nature's messy ways
or awe at the source of life itself …
But no words can penetrate
such frail intimacy
and, as I draw back from the light,
softly closing my fist,
all I can say is:
'I have felt your blood on my hands.'

This and That

This
revolution is like
Passion's flaming fruit
hanging from the tree, glistening,
full-blown with juices that seep out of
the skin to fill the air with the odoriferous
smell of ripe anger, in open defiance of the hungry

gods. But time soon loses interest and passes on,
leaving the withered fruit to the ground, to
rot and decay like bad teeth, and in the
space of a breath all that remains is
dull, compliant and free – fertilizer.
Revolution is like
That

Night above city

Night like clotted
pitch having fallen
into the valley's
street-seared cauldron
was seen by
some to seem
laced, by others
garrotted, by the
city's electrical lines.
This difference of
opinion we left
unresolved, and observed
(silent this time)
the mountain's face
so grotesquely contorted
(by the spotlight
beam projected from
the mountain's base)
as to resemble
pale trees interlocked
by pale shadows.

now and then

poetry is a lonely place:
a secluded courtyard constructed
of ferns reaching out from earth-darkened stone
to blue-deepened moments of sky comes to mind,
but it is always only metaphor and dazed
wanderings across a starch-sterile landscape
where only type can block the nausea,
give the lie to such artificial dreams
of not ever needing all those people now
who won't gather at my bedside then.

TWO POEMS

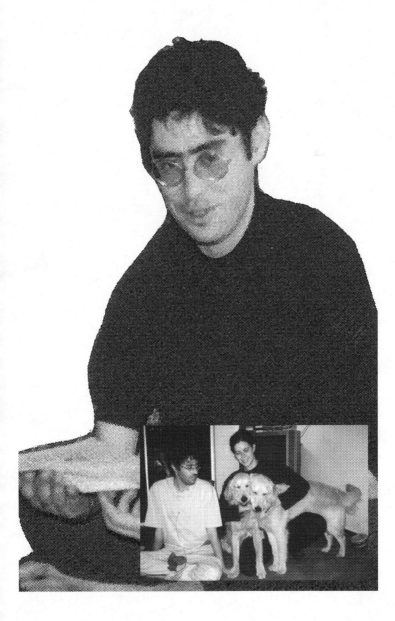

Sisyphus rejoins

None of them cares for me.
They do not know this, but
I overhear them. I hear their
patronising whispers, their conscienceless
conniving to speak of what I do,
to know me.

But what do they know of me?
What can they know of me?
Driven as I am
to push and to push
till sweat gathers on my brow
and limbs, this sweat that is
the lustre of my days
as I push and push,
only and ever to push
to the summit, then down
and back up again, and again,
ever and ever to push …

Yes, none of them cares for me.
What can they – these whisperers –
ever know of a being whose motions
are inscribed in Life, in life
as pattern, blueprint, template.
How can any of these whisperers
match my purpose, my knowing?

To do so would be to know
what they cannot allow themselves
to know – that my motions,

their singularity, show
the truth in all those motions
they call their own –
purposeless, lustreless,
unknowing.

A love letter

Letting go into the freaked-fantastic starlight,
stripped down to the essentials:
skin against the stars,
perfect buttocks, yours, two half moons
caressed by the light of the half moon.
Into the pond, swimming ...

down into the pulsing dark, kelped down,
freed from the clutch of daylight,
down, down into the pulsing dark,
knowing no longer the familiar clutch,
comfort of the light, daylight, moving
only down and down to the source,
to the fear of knowing ...
Knowing what? Knowing you, how
I came to know you – archetype, presence,
dark continent – coming to know
you again and again and again,
down, ever down into the pulsing ...

held, stilled, I came to know you
before I could know or be known,
if you know what I mean,
came to know you back then
before I possessed the apparatus for knowing,
before I could flip and flick, twiddle my dick,
before, before, BC, before the immaculate C.
Now knowing,
let the games commence, let coitus
be non-interruptus, let it be free,
flying freak-fantastic again into the ever and
always starlight when it all began,
to that advent-slime apart from the clutch,

the pall, of daylight, into that deepest dark,
kelped down, down into it again,
pulsing free you and me …

Call it theism of Pan, call it theism of the One
that is I, I as father son and holy ghost,
the I breathing free, hey hallelujah to Me,
sing Me, breathe me, know me ever and always,
amen.
But then what of you? Have you been
forgotten as I backstroke through the tumult
of my god-self rantings, slapping the
little godhead down below into the shine
of his own starlight humming –
hummm … ummm … mmm …
my coming from deep dark to the half-light of day,
to the flexing half-moons, dimpled, silky.
Held there, stilled, known, knowing.

Printed in the United States
by Baker & Taylor Publisher Services